CREATIVE LEATHER JEWELRY

21 STYLISH PROJECTS THAT MAKE A STATEMENT

CREATIVE LEATHER JEWELRY

Christina Anton

LARK
New York

New York

An Imprint of Sterling Publishing Co., Inc.
1166 Avenue of the Americas
New York, NY 10036

ISBN 978-1-4547-0950-3

Distributed in Canada by Sterling Publishing Co., Inc.
c/o Canadian Manda Group, 664 Annette Street
Toronto, Ontario, Canada M6S 2C8
Distributed in the United Kingdom by GMC Distribution Services
Castle Place, 166 High Street, Lewes, East Sussex, England BN7 1XU

For information about custom editions, special sales, and premium and corporate purchases, please
contact Sterling Special Sales at 800-805-5489 or specialsales@sterlingpublishing.com.

Manufactured in China
2 4 6 8 10 9 7 5 3 1

sterlingpublishing.com
larkcrafts.com

Interior design by Amy Trombat

CONTENTS

INTRODUCTION

Welcome to my world of *Creative Leather Jewelry*! I am Christina Anton, an architectural designer turned handmade jewelry business owner from Chicago, Illinois. I love to create bold and unique designs with an emphasis on form, pattern, and color. My jewelry designs are an expression of my background in design and architecture. Using traditional craft techniques and materials, I like to create unique and contemporary pieces of art that you can wear.

Leather is the medium of focus here. One of my favorite aspects of working with leather is its malleable nature. You can easily shape, stamp, cut, dye, paint, and sew it into anything, which is especially great for crafting. The material is durable and long lasting, which adds to the value of goods created from it.

This book pushes the limits of traditional leather craft to create unique and modern works of jewelry. It explores the fundamentals of leather craft while taking a playful twist on technique to create necklaces, earrings, and bracelets you can easily make at home. You can choose to work through the basics step-by-step by taking on each project in order, or you can skip ahead to any project you like and dive right in. All of the steps and templates needed are provided to help you.

Using the techniques taught in the tutorials, the possibilities of where you take leather craft are endless. Whether you are a beginner or advanced, I hope to introduce methods that will spark your creativity and take your jewelry making to the next level.

BASICS

In this section I'll give you all the tools,
techniques, materials, and inspiration you
need to make all of the projects in this book, as
well as the skills to take your jewelry making to
the next level. We'll cover some of my favorite
adornments and techniques that can also be used
in many other forms of jewelry making. The key is
to have fun and let your creativity take over.

TOOLS AND MATERIALS

Leather comes in so many different varieties, but I find that cowhide works best. Cowhide is great because it is thick enough to withstand daily wear and will not lose shape.

For jewelry making purposes, it's not necessary to go into the details of the process of tanning and type. You will be using genuine leather that is dyed in a variety of colors. Pretty much any leather you search for that is dyed will be adequate. For small-scale jewelry projects, you don't need the highest grade leather. For these purposes consistency and color are the most important factors in choosing a hide.

Grain is an important factor when selecting a hide. I personally like the natural grain and blemish of original hides as it adds to the texture of the jewelry.

There are also smoother options to choose from if you would like a more minimal, less textured look.

I find that a thickness of $^1/_{32}$ inch to $^3/_{32}$ inch (1 mm to 2 mm) is easier to hand cut and manipulate. Hides that are too thick will be harder to cut and assemble. If a leather hide is very thin, it can be glued with leather glue to make a double layer.

Weight Classifications of Leather

Many leather suppliers classify the leather by weight:

1 ounce	$^1/_{64}$ inch (0.4 mm)
2 ounce	$^1/_{32}$ inch (0.8 mm)
3 ounce	$^3/_{64}$ inch (1.2 mm)
4 ounce	$^1/_{16}$ inch (1.6 mm)
5 ounce	$^5/_{64}$ inch (2 mm)
6 ounce	$^3/_{32}$ inch (2.4 mm)
7 ounce	$^7/_{64}$ inch (2.8 mm)
8 ounce	$^1/_8$ inch (3.2 mm)

The most common sizes are 1- to 3-ounce leather thicknesses; these will work very well for most projects. Any thickness beyond 8 ounces might be too difficult to cut by hand.

A **rotary leather hole punch** is a tool to help make different sized holes in your creations. It is made up of six bell punches that you rotate depending on the size you need. I like to use this tool to create holes in the leather and then attach jewelry findings quickly and easily.

Vegan options are available if you are opposed to using genuine leather and would like a more animal friendly choice. Faux or artificial leather is made of synthetic fibers, such as plastic or PVC, while still maintaining material qualities similar to real leather. The benefits of faux leather are lower cost and easy access to bright and neon colors.

Feathers are one of my favorite materials to use. I find that they add interesting texture and color to my creations. I use dyed goose feathers because they have a great shape and they are large. It is best to start with a large fuller feather and then trim as needed.

Cutting mats are a great way to protect your work surface and keep cutting blades sharp. The best mats are self-healing and come in a variety of sizes. I usually use a mat size of 24 × 36 inches (61.0 × 91.4 cm.) For the projects in this book, a small mat 8 × 11 inches (20.3 × 27.9 cm) can be used.

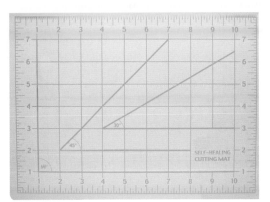

Cutting knives are the most important tool in leather craft. A great knife and blade will help you to achieve accuracy in your designs. You also want a good blade for reliability and safety. The type of knife and blade to use will depend on your comfort level and experience.

Leather glue and **cyanoacrylate glue** will be used for the projects in this book and will be listed in the materials list when they are needed.

Round-nose pliers will be used in making wire loops. They have a tapered design that allows you to control the size of loop needed.

Chain-nose pliers are one of my frequently used tools. They have a flat surface which works great to open and close jump rings. I really like the pliers that have a side cutter inlay that can cut wire. If your pliers have this feature, you will not need separate wire-cutter pliers.

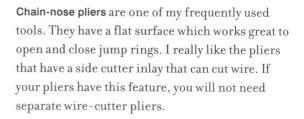

Wire-cutter pliers are used to cut metal jewelry findings such as head pins, eye pins, and necklace chain.

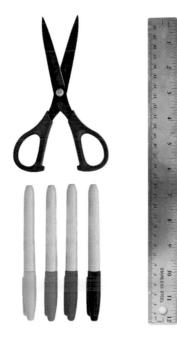

JEWELRY FINDINGS

Jump rings are a metal ring made of wire in a circular shape that has a break or opening in the ring. They are used to connect elements together. I prefer to use a 6-mm ring for connecting leather elements and a 4-mm size ring to attach earring hooks or lobster clasps. See the proper way to open and close jump rings in the techniques section (page 9).

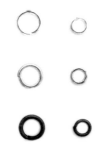

Miscellaneous other tools that you may need include scissors, a ruler, and disappearing fabric markers. Make sure that you select scissors that are very sharp to cut through the leather. Some of the shapes in the templates are easier to cut with scissors than with a cutting knife. It will depend on what works best for you.

Ear wires come in a variety of designs and finishes. Different types of ear wires include kidney, post and stud, fish hook, hoop and lever back. My favorite earring findings are French hooks because they have a clean look and are easy to attach. You can select whichever kind you like.

Head pins are thin wires with a flat end to keep beads in place. You can slide beads and other gemstones onto the wire and then finish it with a loop to keep them from falling off. Head pins have only one connection to your jewelry. When your beads are finished with a loop they are ready to be attached to the leather. I find that a 21-gauge thickness works best because it is sturdy and easy to loop.

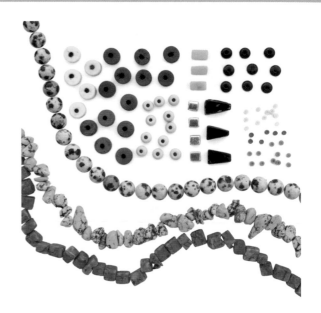

Eye pins are a thin wire that has a loop on each end. They are used to attach multiple pieces together. Eye pins can be connected to your jewelry at both ends.

Beads and **gemstones** will be used to add more style to your designs. I like to use seed beads because they come in almost any color you can imagine. I also love gemstone beads, such as jasper, turquoise, and onyx, that come in different shapes and sizes. You can go to your local craft store to select beads you like or shop online.

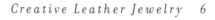

Necklace chain is made up of several links that come in a variety of metals. I personally love to use curb chain with a link size of ⅛ × ⅛ inch (3 × 3 mm). Metals that I frequently use include brass, silver-plated brass, and gold-plated brass. To reduce skin allergies, I only use chain that is nickel and lead free; it can be worn with sensitive skin.

Crimp ends are used to finish the ends of your jewelry with a professional look. Crimp ends work well for finishing the end of feathers. See the techniques section for how to properly use a crimp end.

Ribbon ends are a larger version of crimp ends and can be used to hold larger pieces of leather together. Some of these projects require 1-inch (2.5 cm) ribbon ends. To use simply insert the material into the end and clamp down with chain-nose pliers.

Lobster clasps are added to the ends of the necklace chain to finish off a necklace. The clasp has a lever that opens and closes so that the necklace can be worn securely.

HOW TO USE A CUTTING BLADE

The secret to holding a cutting blade correctly is to hold it almost as you would hold a pen or pencil. It takes some practice to get used to the grip and to find the right position that works for you. To help steady your hand, lean your wrist on a flat surface.

As you cut your material, try to keep the blade perpendicular to the surface to make sure you are getting clean 90-degree cuts.

HOLE PUNCHING

To punch holes, hold a piece of leather under the hole stamp of your choice. Simply hold your piece of leather steady as you close the stamp lightly to see exactly where the hole will be.

Once you are happy with the placement, squeeze the punch and your hole will be placed. Rotary punches usually have about six different-sized holes to choose from. For making jewelry, you will be using the smallest one.

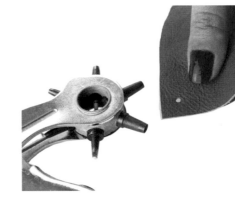

OPENING AND CLOSING JUMP RINGS

Opening and closing jump rings are achieved by using two pairs of chain-nose pliers. To properly open and close the rings, you do not pull them apart.

You hold a jump ring with one pliers on each side of the break in the ring. Push one pliers forward while holding the other in place.

The twist motion is key in opening and closing the rings to ensure that they do not lose their shape.

To close, twist the ends back until the jump ring is closed.

MAKING LOOPS

To make a loop, string several beads onto the head pin or eye pin.

You will need about ¼ inch (6 mm) of the pin left after your beads are added. Next you will use round-nose pliers to pull the pin into a 90-degree angle at the top of the beads.

Use the round-nose pliers to loop the pin around into a circle that ends where you started. You can use your pliers to adjust the pin if you cannot get a perfect circle.

HOW TO CAP FEATHERS FOR JEWELRY USE
Some of these projects use feathers to make earrings and necklaces. A leather crimp can be added to the top of unfinished feathers for a more finished look.

First, prepare the feather by trimming it at the top to leave a small amount of stem. To use a crimp end, place it flat on your surface with the two open ends facing you.

Place your feather into the crimp, and add a little bit of cyanoacrylate glue to keep it in place.

Once the glue is set, use your chain-nose pliers to push the ends of the crimp one at a time inwards.

PROJECTS

GEOMETRIC CUTOUT EARRINGS

⚡⚡

CREATE GEOMETRIC DANGLE EARRINGS USING A
SIMPLE DESIGN THAT MAKES A BOLD STATEMENT.
HAND CUT BRIGHT LEATHER, AND ATTACH THE
VARIOUS PIECES USING JUMP RINGS.

1 Gather all of the materials and tools needed. One color or several color leathers can be used to make the earrings. For this project I have selected three different colors.

2 Copy shapes A, B, and C from template 1 on a separate sheet of paper. Then cut out the shapes using a cutting blade or scissors. Each of the three shapes in the template is used twice to create two earrings. Make sure to stamp out the holes on the template.

3 Cut out one earring using the shapes A, B, and C from the template. Start by placing shape A on the leather and tracing around it using a cutting blade. Repeat for shapes B and C.

MATERIALS

- Template 1 (page 106)
- Leather
- 6 jump rings, 6 mm
- 2 jump rings, 4 mm
- 1 pair of ear wires

TOOLS

- 1 cutting knife
- Cutting blades
- 1 cutting mat
- 2 chain-nose pliers
- 1 disappearing fabric marker
- 1 rotary hole punch

4 Continue cutting the leather using the templates for the second earring. You will end up with a total of six shapes.

5 Using a disappearing fabric marker, create marks on the leather where the holes will be stamped. Note that shape C only has one hole because it will be the bottom piece.

6 Use the rotary hole punch to create holes where previously marked.

7 Continue to punch all holes until your pieces are complete.

8 Use the 6-mm jump rings to attach each piece to the next with A at the top, B in the middle, and C at the bottom. Repeat for the second earring. Be sure to add a 6-mm jump ring at the top of A so the ear wire can be attached.

9 Once the geometric leather pieces are attached with jump rings, attach a 4-mm jump ring to the 6-mm jump ring at the top of A, and add an ear wire. Repeat for the second earring.

GEOMETRIC CUTOUT EARRINGS WITH EMBELLISHMENTS

THESE EARRINGS COMBINE THE FUNDAMENTAL CUTOUT
TECHNIQUE USED THROUGHOUT THE PROJECTS WITH
SMALLER DANGLING GEOMETRIC PIECES. IT
MAKES A BOLD EFFECT.

1 Gather all of the materials and tools needed. To make the design really unique choose several different colors of leather.

2 Copy shapes A, B, and C from template 2 on a separate sheet of paper. Then cut out the shapes using a cutting blade or scissors. Stamp out the holes on the template for future markings.

3 Place the templates on the leather, and cut each shape out very carefully. Shapes A and B are used twice to create a total of four pieces.

MATERIALS

◆ Template 2 (page 106)
◆ Leather
◆ 20 jump rings, 6 mm
◆ 2 jump rings, 4 mm
◆ 1 pair of ear wires

TOOLS

◆ 1 cutting knife
◆ Cutting blades
◆ 1 cutting mat
◆ 2 chain-nose pliers
◆ 1 disappearing fabric marker
◆ 1 rotary hole punch

4 Shape C is used to cut out the 14 tear drops that dangle at the bottom of the earrings.

5 Use a disappearing marker to transfer the placement of the holes from the template shapes to each of the pieces of leather. The marks will show where to punch the holes for the jump rings.

6 Punch through each mark using the rotary hole punch. Place the marked leather under the smallest hole of the rotary hole punch, and squeeze to pierce through the leather. Continue to punch all 38 holes.

7 After the holes are punched, begin assembling the earrings using jump rings.

8 Start by adding 6-mm jump rings to attach shape A to shape B using a pair of chain-nose pliers. Add a jump ring to the top of shape A so that the ear wires can be attached in the last step.

9 Attach all the shape Cs to the bottom of the shape Bs using 14 jump rings. Each earring will have seven dangling pieces.

10 Add an ear wire to the top 6-mm jump ring at the top of A using a 4-mm jump ring. Repeat for the second earring.

11 The earrings are now complete and ready to wear! I used three different colors of leather for this project. A variation would be to choose multiple colors for the dangling pieces to add even more color.

LEATHER TASSEL EARRINGS

LEARN THE BASICS OF TASSEL MAKING AND CREATE A STYLISH STATEMENT EARRING. THE DESIGN CAN BE MADE UNIQUE BY CHOOSING DIFFERENT COLORS OF LEATHER FOR EACH TASSEL OR ONE SHADE FOR ALL TASSELS.

1 Gather all of the materials and tools listed.

2 Copy shapes A, B, and C from template 3 on a separate sheet of paper. Then cut out the shapes using a cutting blade or scissors. Note the pink dotted lines that can be used as a guide when measuring tassel cuts.

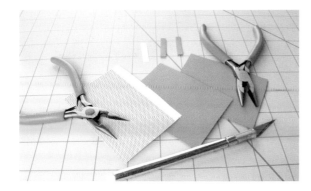

3 Place shapes A and B on top of the leather and cut around. Shape A is the leather tassel, and shape B is the attachment that the jump ring will hang from. Repeat for the second earring for a total of four cutouts.

MATERIALS

- Template 3 (page 106)
- Leather
- 2 jump rings, 6 mm
- 2 jump rings, 4 mm
- 1 pair of ear wires

TOOLS

- 1 cutting knife
- Cutting blades
- 1 cutting mat
- 2 chain-nose pliers
- 1 disappearing fabric marker
- 1 ruler
- Cyanoacrylate glue
- Leather bond glue

4 Using a disappearing fabric marker and a ruler, or the pink dashed lines on the template, make small marks along the bottom edge of the back side of the leather at each ¹⁄₁₆ inch (1.5 mm). Marking on the back side prevents the marks from showing on the finished side. The ¹⁄₁₆-inch (1.5 mm) marks determine the width of each strand of the tassel. Feel free to make the cuts wider or narrower depending on preference.

5 Again working on the back side of the leather, measure down from the top edge ¼ inch (6 mm), and draw a very light line with the disappearing marker. Along this line make ¹⁄₁₆-inch (1.5 mm) marks corresponding to the marks made along the bottom edge.

6 With the ruler, cut parallel, straight lines from the top marks to the bottom marks and through the bottom edge. Make sure *not* to cut all the way to the top.

7 Repeat to create two tassels. If the guide marks made from steps 4 and 5 are visible, use a cutting blade to scrape them off.

8 Working on the back side of the leather, align one short end of shape B on the top left edge of the tassel cutout, and use cyanoacrylate glue to adhere. Fold shape B in half to create a loop and glue again. The loop is used to connect the jump ring and ear wire to the tassel. Repeat for the second tassel.

9 On the back side of the leather, spread a narrow band of leather bond glue along the top edge of the tassel cutout stopping ¼ inch (6 mm) from the end. This helps to strengthen the tassel. Hold the top of the loop, and roll tightly to create the tassel. Keep rolling until ¼ inch (6 mm) is left. Add cyanoacrylate glue to the end, and finish rolling. The glue will help keep the tassel from unrolling. Repeat for the second tassel.

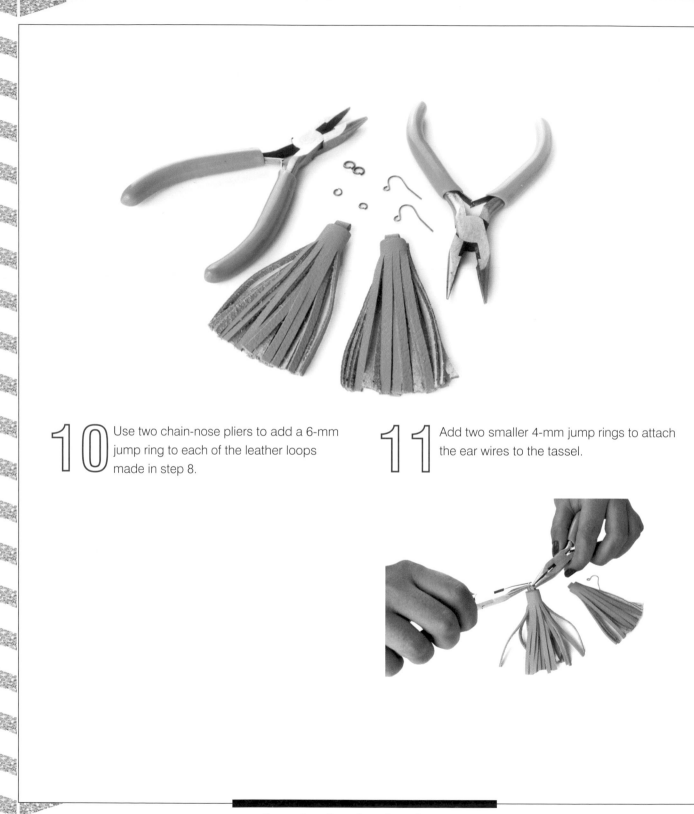

10 Use two chain-nose pliers to add a 6-mm jump ring to each of the leather loops made in step 8.

11 Add two smaller 4-mm jump rings to attach the ear wires to the tassel.

DOUBLE LAYER VARIATION

1 Repeat steps 4 through 7 using shape C from the template. This piece will be added to the tassel to create a double-layer tassel.

2 Repeat step 9 rolling shape C onto the already finished shape A. Trim away any overlap if needed. Repeat for the second tassel.

GEOMETRIC FRINGE
LEATHER EARRINGS

ᔓ ᔒ

COMBINE A FUN FRINGED LOOK WITH GEOMETRIC
CUTOUT ELEMENTS. USE THE TASSEL TECHNIQUE
AND CUT OUT A GEOMETRIC LATTICE TO HANG
IN FRONT OF THE FRINGE.

Gather all of the materials and tools listed.

2 Copy shapes A, B, C, D, and E from template 4 on a separate sheet of paper. Then cut out the shapes using a cutting blade or scissors. The project requires one each of shapes A, B, C, and D and two cutouts of shape E to make a pair of earrings. Note the pink dotted lines that can be used as a guide for shape E. Remember to punch the holes as marked on the templates.

MATERIALS

- Template 4 (page 107)
- Leather
- 2 jump rings, 6 mm
- 2 jump rings, 4 mm
- 1 pair of ear wires

TOOLS

- 1 cutting knife
- Cutting blades
- 1 cutting mat
- 2 chain-nose pliers
- 1 disapparing fabric marker
- 1 ruler
- 1 rotary hole punch

3 Place shapes A, B, C, and D on top of the leather and cut around. Shape E is used twice to create two fringe pieces. If shapes C and D are too complicated to cut out, use only the outline to cut around the outside of the shape and do not cut out the centers.

4 For each shape E, working on the back side of the leather, use a ruler to make marks every $\frac{1}{16}$ inch (1.5 mm) along the bottom edge (or use the template as a guide). Measure halfway up the shape, and, with a disappearing fabric marker, make marks every $\frac{1}{16}$ inch (1.5 mm) to correspond with the marks along the bottom edge. Using the ruler to ensure parallel, straight lines, cut the shape to create fringe.

5 Use a marker to transfer all holes that will be punched in the next step. Shapes C and D do not need a hole punch because of the geometric cut outs. However if you chose not to cut out the center in step 3, you will need to create a hole in the top point of each shape.

6 Punch through each mark using the rotary hole punch. Place the leather under the smallest hole, and squeeze to pierce through the leather.

8 Attach with pliers a 4-mm jump ring and the ear wire to each earring.

7 Arrange the cutouts for the first earring face up on top of each other with shape E on the bottom, shape B in the middle, and shape D on top. Align the holes, and use two chain-nose pliers to join the pieces together with a 6-mm jump ring. Repeat for the second earring, placing shape E on the bottom, shape A in the middle, and shape C on top.

GEOMETRIC DANGLE
STATEMENT EARRINGS

THESE GEOMETRIC STATEMENT EARRINGS COMBINE
A LAYERING OF DIFFERENT SHAPES WITH DANGLING
EMBELLISHMENTS FOR A BOLD LOOK. THE VARIOUS
COLORS OF LEATHER AND FUN HAND-CUT FORMS
MAKE THIS DESIGN REALLY STAND OUT.

1 Gather all of the materials and tools listed.

2 Copy shapes A, B, C, D, and E from template 5 on a separate sheet of paper. Then cut out the shapes using a cutting blade or scissors. The template requires 2 each of shapes A, B, C, and D, 4 cutouts of shape D, and 12 cutouts of shape E to make a pair of earrings. Punch through the holes on the template shapes.

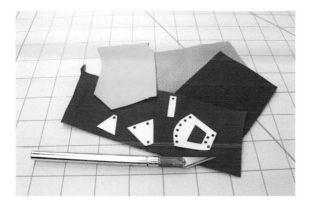

3 Place shapes A, B, C, D, and E on the leather and cut around. Use a marker to trace shapes onto the leather if needed.

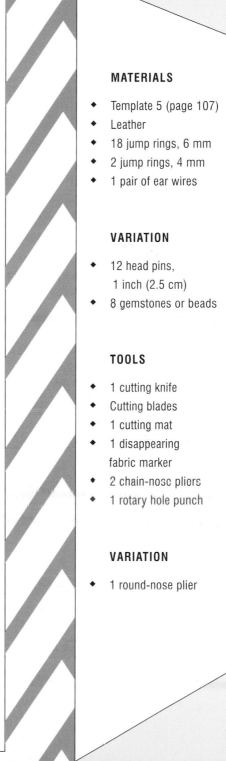

MATERIALS

- Template 5 (page 107)
- Leather
- 18 jump rings, 6 mm
- 2 jump rings, 4 mm
- 1 pair of ear wires

VARIATION

- 12 head pins,
  1 inch (2.5 cm)
- 8 gemstones or beads

TOOLS

- 1 cutting knife
- Cutting blades
- 1 cutting mat
- 1 disappearing
  fabric marker
- 2 chain-nose pliers
- 1 rotary hole punch

VARIATION

- 1 round-nose plier

4 Use a disappearing fabric marker to mark the holes in the templates. The holes will determine where to punch using the rotary hole punch.

7 Start by attaching shape A to shape B using two 6-mm jump rings. Use the pairs of pliers to attach the rings.

8 Attach shape C to shape A also a 6-mm jump ring..

5 Punch through each mark using the rotary hole punch. Place the leather under the smallest hole, and squeeze to pierce through the leather. Continue to punch all 44 holes.

9 Using 6-mm jump rings, add the embellishment shape D to the middle of shape B. Finish off the earring by attaching 6 of shape D to the bottom of shape B.

6 To begin assembly, gather the jump rings, ear wires, and two chain-nose pliers.

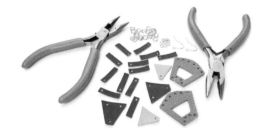

10 Repeat steps 7 through 9 for the second earring by attaching all templates using 6-mm jump rings.

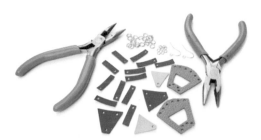

11 At the top of A attach a 4-mm jump ring and an ear wire, and repeat for the second earring.

VARIATION

1 You may substitute beads or other materials for shapes D and E. Here I have used the gemstones jasper, howlite, and onyx to create an embellished look. Start by stringing beads onto the head pins and looping the end. The beads that dangle at the bottom of shape B can be as large as needed. The beads dangling in the middle of shape B need to be small enough to fit inside the cut out.

2 Attach all beads using 6-mm jump rings just as in step 9.

DANGLE TASSEL EARRINGS

THIS PROJECT IS FOR THE TASSEL LOVER. MAKE
EARRINGS WITH MULTIPLE HANDCUT LEATHER TASSELS
THAT DANGLE FROM CHAINS AT DIFFERENT LENGTHS.
THIS IS A GREAT DESIGN TO REALLY PLAY WITH COLOR
VARIATIONS FOR A UNIQUE LOOK.

Gather all of the materials and tools listed.

2 Copy shapes A and B from template 6 on a separate sheet of paper. Then cut out the shapes using a cutting blade or scissors.. Shapes A and B are used to cut six leather tassels.

3 Place shapes A and B on the leather and cut around the template. Continue to cut until there are six of shape A and six of shape B.

MATERIALS

- Template 6 (page 107)
- Leather
- 11 inches (28 cm) curb chain
- 2 jump rings, 6 mm
- 8 jump rings, 4 mm
- 1 pair of ear wires

TOOLS

- 1 cutting knife
- Cutting blades
- 1 cutting mat
- 1 disappearing fabric marker
- 1 ruler
- 2 chain-nose pliers
- 1 wire-cutter pliers
- Cyanoacrylate glue
- Leather bond glue

4 On each of the tassel pieces, measure down 1/8 inch (3 mm) from the top edge, and make a row of marks 1/16 inch (1.5 mm) apart along this line. Next, with a disappearing fabric marker make a corresponding set of 1/16-inch (1.5 mm) marks along the bottom edge. Cut the tassels beginning at the top mark and cutting through the bottom of the shape. Make sure not to mark or cut all the way to the top edge because a top strip is needed to roll the piece into a tassel in future steps.

5 Using a ruler, cut the tassels in parallel, straight lines from the top mark through the bottom until all of shape A is cut.

6 Repeat five more times on the remaining A shapes.

7 Use cyanoacrylate glue to adhere shape B onto the upper right hand side of the tassel. Fold shape B down to create a loop, and glue once more. The loop will be used to attach the tassel with a jump ring to the chain.

8 Add leather bond glue along the top from left to right, and begin to roll the tassel. Make sure to use the index and thumb fingers to guide the tassel so that the top is straight and even.

9 Repeat steps 7 and 8 for each of the remaining A shapes. The tassels are complete and ready to be added to the chain.

10 Measure out six pieces of chain, and cut using wire-cutter pliers. Two pieces measure 3 inches (7.6 cm) long, two pieces are 1½ inches (3.8 cm) long, and two pieces are 1 inch (2.5 cm) long.

11 Lay out the tassels and chain lengths for each earring. For a symmetrical look match the color of tassel with the same length chain for each earring.

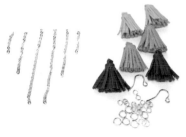

12 Using 4-mm jump rings and a two chain-nose pliers hang one tassel in the middle of each of the six chains.

13 One earring will be composed of hanging a 1-inch (2.5 cm), 1½-inch (3.8 cm), and 3-inch (7.6 cm) chain in order from shortest to longest onto a 6-mm jump ring. Slip each end of the tassel's chain onto the jump ring before adding the next tassel. Repeat for the other earring, reversing the order in which you add the tassels.

14 Lastly, add a 4-mm jump ring to attach an ear wire for both earrings.

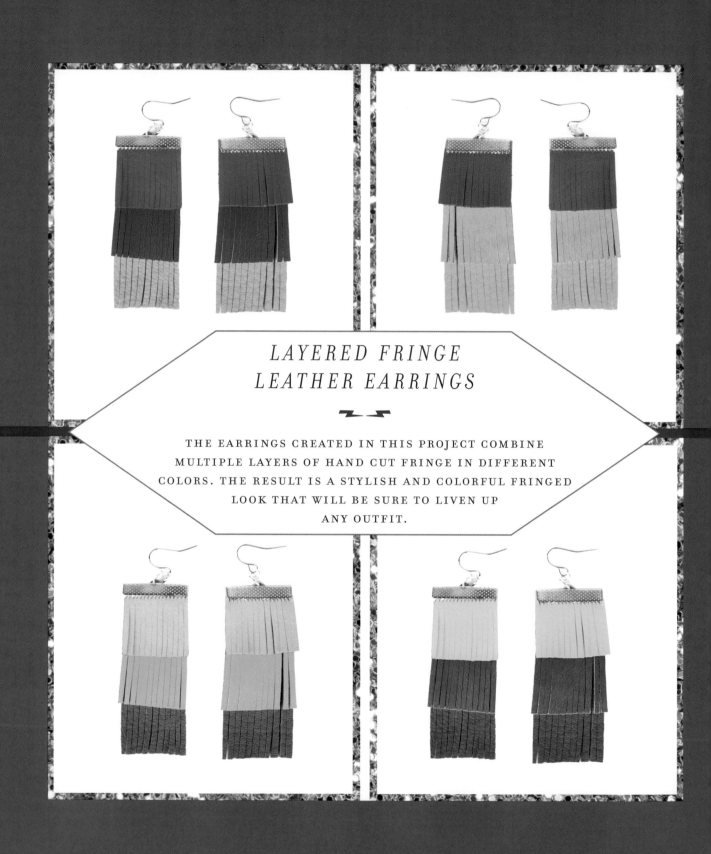

LAYERED FRINGE LEATHER EARRINGS

THE EARRINGS CREATED IN THIS PROJECT COMBINE
MULTIPLE LAYERS OF HAND CUT FRINGE IN DIFFERENT
COLORS. THE RESULT IS A STYLISH AND COLORFUL FRINGED
LOOK THAT WILL BE SURE TO LIVEN UP
ANY OUTFIT.

Gather all of the materials and tools listed.

Copy shapes A, B, and C from template 7 on a separate sheet of paper. Then cut out the shapes using a cutting blade or scissors. Each shape is used twice to create a total of six pieces.

Place shapes A, B, and C over the leather, and cut each shape out. The selection of colors used can be customized to create a unique look. For this project, I used three colors, a different one for each layer of fringe.

MATERIALS

- Template 7 (page 108)
- Leather
- 2 jump rings, 6 mm
- 2 jump rings, 4 mm
- 2 ribbon ends,
  1 inch (2.5 cm)
- 1 pair of ear wires

TOOLS

- 1 cutting knife
- Cutting blades
- 1 cutting mat
- 1 disappearing
  fabric marker
- 1 ruler
- 2 chain-nose pliers
- Cyanoacrylate glue

4 On each of the fringe pieces, measure down ⅛ inch (3 mm) from the top edge, and make a row of marks ¹⁄₁₆ inch (1.5 mm) apart along this line. Next, with a disappearing fabric marker make a corresponding set of ¹⁄₁₆-inch (1.5 mm) marks along the bottom edge. Cut the fringes beginning at the top mark and cutting through the bottom of the shape. Use a ruler to make sure the cuts are parallel and straight. Make sure not to mark or cut all the way to the top edge.

5 Repeat step 4 for each of the remaining fringe pieces.

6 To begin assembling the earrings, align the fringe pieces face up on top of each other. Place shape C on the bottom, shape B in the middle, and shape A on top, making sure that they meet evenly at the top. Repeat for the second earring. This will create the layered fringe look.

Run a line of cyanoacrylate glue inside the 1-inch (2.5 cm) ribbon end to keep the earrings more secure. Place the ribbon end over the top edge of the stacked leather pieces, and use the chain-nose pliers to clamp it shut. Make sure that the earrings are evenly aligned so that each fringe layer is straight. Repeat for the second earring.

Using a pair of chain-nose pliers, add a 6-mm jump ring to each earring.

Lastly, connect a 4-mm jump ring to the 6-mm ring, and attach the ear wire for both pairs.

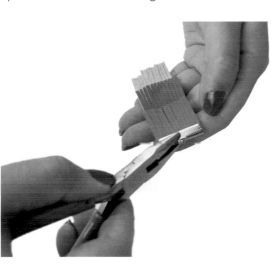

GEOMETRIC EARRINGS
WITH SMALL TASSELS

LIKE THE GEOMETRIC FRINGE EARRINGS, THESE
EARRINGS COMBINE COLORFUL CUTOUTS WITH
SIX TINY HANGING TASSELS.

Gather all of the materials and tools listed.

 Copy shapes A, B, C, D, and E from template 8 on a separate sheet of paper. Then cut out the shapes using a cutting blade or scissors. Shapes A, B, and C are used twice to create a total of six pieces for the upper part of the earrings. Shapes D and E are used six times to create a total of six tassels that will hang below the earrings. Punch out the holes in the template shapes.

Place all shapes over the leather and use as a guide to cut out each template.

MATERIALS

* Template 8 (page 108)
* Leather
* 8 jump rings, 6 mm
* 2 jump rings, 4 mm
* 1 pair of ear wires

TOOLS

* 1 cutting knife
* Cutting blades
* 1 cutting mat
* 1 disappearing fabric marker
* 1 ruler
* 2 chain-nose pliers
* 1 rotary hole punch
* Cyanoacrylate glue
* Leather bond glue

4 Use a disappearing fabric marker to mark each hole in shapes A, B, and C.

5 Punch through each mark using the rotary hole punch. Place the leather under the smallest hole, and squeeze to pierce through the leather. Continue to punch all 12 holes.

6 Next prepare the tassels using shapes D and E. On each of the tassel pieces, measure down ⅛ inch (3 mm) from the top edge, and, with a disappearing fabric marker, make a row of marks 1/16 inch (1.5 mm) apart along this line. Next mark a corresponding set of 1/16-inch (1.5 mm) marks along the bottom edge. Cut the tassels beginning at the top mark and cutting through the bottom of shape. Use a ruler to make sure the cuts are parallel and straight. Make sure not to mark or cut all the way to the top edge because a top strip is needed to roll the piece into a tassel in future steps. Repeat to create six tassels.

7 Use cyanoacrylate glue to adhere shape E to the top left corner. Fold the strip down to create a loop, and glue again. On the back side of the leather, spread a narrow band of leather bond glue along the top edge of the tassel cutout stopping ¼ inch (6 mm) from the end. This helps to strengthen the tassel. Hold the top of the loop, and roll tightly to create the tassel. Keep rolling until ¼ inch (6 mm) is left. Add cyanoacrylate glue to the end, and finish rolling. The glue will help keep the tassel from unrolling.

8 Repeat step 7 with each of the remaining tassel pieces.

9 Add the tassels to the bottom of shape B using a two chain-nose pliers and 6-mm jump rings. Continue until all six tassels, three on each earring, are attached.

10 Add shapes A and C to the top hole in shape B using pliers and 6-mm jump rings. Finally, add a 4-mm jump ring and an ear wire to both earrings.

DANGLING CHAIN LEATHER EARRINGS

⚡

THIS PROJECT INTRODUCES A NEW TECHNIQUE
USING CHAINS AS THE MAIN DESIGN ELEMENT.
DIFFERENT LENGTH CHAINS DANGLE FROM A
GEOMETRIC LEATHER CUTOUT, WHICH MAKES
A BOLD STATEMENT EARRING.

1 Gather all of the materials and tools listed.

2 Copy shapes A and B from template 9 on a separate sheet of paper. Then cut out the shapes using a cutting blade or scissors. Shapes A and B are cut twice for a total of four pieces. Punch the holes in the template shapes.

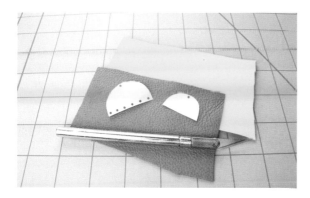

3 Put shapes A and B over the leather and cut around each template.

MATERIALS

- Template 9 (page 108)
- Leather
- Curb chain, 18 inches (45.7 cm)
- 14 jump rings, 6 mm
- 2 jump rings, 4 mm
- 1 pair of ear wires

TOOLS

- 1 cutting knife
- Cutting blades
- 1 cutting mat
- 1 disappearing fabric marker
- 1 ruler
- 1 wire-cutter pliers
- 2 chain-nose pliers
- 1 rotary hole punch

4 Use a disappearing fabric marker to mark all small circles of the template onto the leather. These holes will be punched in the next step.

6 Prepare to assemble the earrings by selecting the style of chain you desire. I used silver-plated bronze curb chain with links sized 3 mm × 3 mm.

5 Punch through each mark using the rotary hole punch. Place the leather under the smallest hole, and squeeze to pierce through the leather. Continue to punch all 16 holes.

7 Measure out six pieces of chain, and cut using wire-cutter pliers. Two pieces should measure 4 inches (10.2 cm) long, two should be 3 inches (7.6 cm) long, and two should be 2 inches (5.1 cm) long.

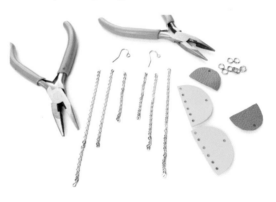

8 Taking the longest 4-inch (10.2 cm) chain, attach one end to each of the outer left and right holes of shape B using 6-mm jump rings and two chain-nose pliers. Next attach each end of the 3-inch (7.6 cm) chain to the next holes inward. Lastly, attach the 2-inch (5.1 cm) chain to the two middle holes of shape B. The longest chain loops from one outside hole to the other, and the chain loops decrease in size toward the middle.

10 Position shape A on top of shape B aligning the holes. Attach a 6-mm jump ring at the top to connect shapes A and B together. A will hang over B. Take a 4-mm jump ring and attach to the top 6-mm jump ring to attach the ear wire.

9 Repeat step 8 for the second earring.

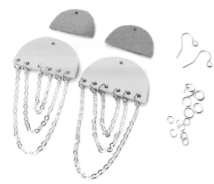

LEATHER AND
FEATHER EARRINGS

THESE EARRINGS COMBINE MULTIPLE MATERIALS
AND TECHNIQUES TO CREATE AN ECLECTIC DESIGN.
MY FAVORITE MATERIALS TO USE ARE A COMBINATION
OF COLORFUL GEOMETRIC LEATHER CUTOUTS AND
BRIGHT FEATHERS BECAUSE THEY MAKE A
BOLD AND DISTINCTIVE STATEMENT PIECE.

Gather all of the materials and tools listed.

2 Copy shapes A and B from template 10 on a separate sheet of paper. Then cut out the shapes using a cutting blade or scissors Shapes A and B are cut twice for a total of four pieces. Punch the holes marked on the template shapes.

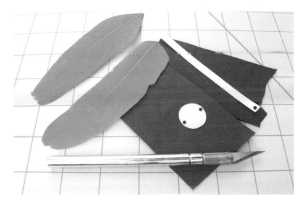

3 Place shape A and B on top of the leather, and cut around the template using a cutting knife and blade.

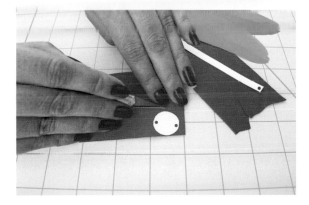

MATERIALS

- Template 10 (page 109)
- Leather
- 2 Feathers
- 2 crimp ends
- 4 jump rings, 6 mm
- 2 jump rings, 4 mm
- 1 pair of ear wires

TOOLS

- 1 cutting knife
- Cutting blades
- 1 cutting mat
- 1 disappearing fabric marker
- 2 chain-nose pliers
- 1 wire-cutter pliers
- 1 rotary hole punch
- Cyanoacrylate glue

4 Use a disappearing fabric marker to mark all small circles of the template onto the leather. These marks act as a guide for the next step.

5 Punch through each mark using the rotary hole punch. Place the leather under the smallest hole, and squeeze to pierce through the leather. Continue to punch all six holes in shapes A and B.

6 To prepare the feather for capping, use a cutting blade to remove feathers from the upper stem, removing about ¼ inch (6.4 mm) from the top.

7 Put the trimmed stem into the crimp end with the ends facing up. Add a bit of cyanoacrylate glue to strengthen the hold into the crimp end. Use a pair of chain-nose pliers to push the ends of the crimp flat to overlap the stem.

8 Repeat steps 6 and 7 for the second feather.

10 Attach a 4-mm jump ring to the top 6-mm jump ring of A, and add an ear wire. Repeat for the second earring.

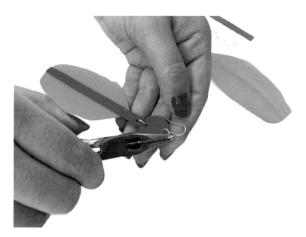

9 Combine the feather, shape B, and shape A using chain-nosed pliers and a 6-mm jump ring. The order should be the feather in the back, shape B next, and shape A on top. Add another 6-mm jump ring to the top of shape A. Repeat for the second earring.

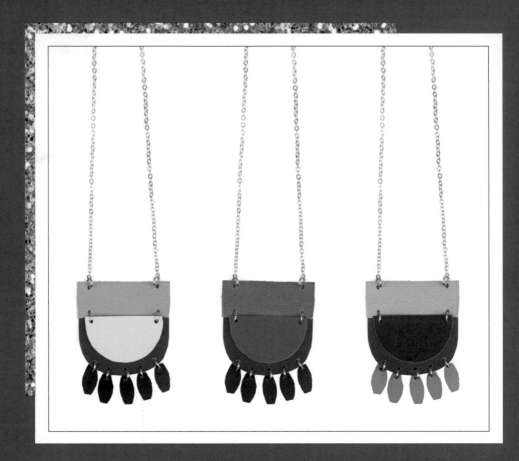

CRESCENT GEOMETRIC
LEATHER NECKLACE

CREATE A FUN STATEMENT NECKLACE USING LAYERED
GEOMETRIC CUTOUTS WITH SMALL EMBELLISHMENTS.
HAVE FUN CHOOSING BRIGHT AND UNEXPECTED COLOR
COMBINATIONS TO PERSONALIZE THE DESIGN.

1 Gather all of the materials and tools listed.

2 Copy shapes A, B, C, and D from template 11 on a separate sheet of paper. Then cut out the shapes using a cutting blade or scissors. Shape D is used to cut five pieces. Punch out the holes marked on the template shapes.

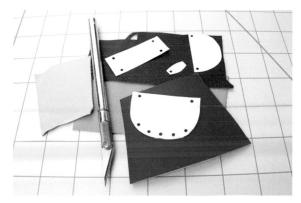

3 Place shapes A, B, C, and D on top of the leather using the template as a guide to cut around. Replace the blade as needed to get clean and precise cuts.

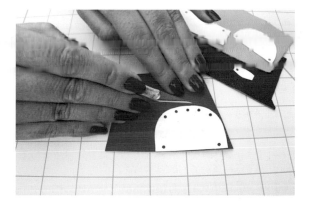

MATERIALS

- Template 11 (page 109)
- Leather
- 10 jump rings, 6 mm
- 1 jump ring, 4 mm
- 1 necklace chain, 20 inches (50.8 cm) long
- 1 lobster clasp

TOOLS

- 1 cutting knife
- Cutting blades
- 1 cutting mat
- 1 disappearing fabric marker
- 1 ruler
- 2 chain-nose pliers
- 1 wire-cutter pliers
- 1 rotary hole punch

4 Use a disappearing fabric marker to mark the small circles of the template onto the leather. The marks serve as a guide for the next step.

6 Measure out two pieces of curb chain 10 inches (25.4 cm) long, and use the wire-cutter pliers to cut each chain.

5 Punch through each mark using the rotary hole punch. Place the leather under the smallest hole and squeeze to pierce through the leather. Continue to punch all 28 holes in the shapes.

7 Start assembling the leather necklace by attaching five pieces of shape D to the bottom holes in shape B. Use 6-mm jump rings with a pair of chain-nosed pliers. Repeat for the second earring.

Attach shape A in front of shape B, and add shape C to the top using 6-mm jump rings.

Using 6-mm jump rings, attach one chain to the top left hole of shape C, and attach the other chain piece to the top right hole of shape C.

10 To finish the necklace, use a 4-mm jump ring to attach a lobster clasp to the chain on one side. Add a 6-mm jump ring to the end of the chain on the other side. The lobster clasp closes into the jump ring, and the necklace is complete.

GEOMETRIC TASSEL NECKLACE

CREATE A LAYERED GEOMETRIC NECKLACE WITH
TASSELS. A TOUCH OF METALLIC LEATHER CAN MAKE
ANY DESIGN HAVE A HIGH-END LOOK. I LIKE TO USE
MULTIPLE SHADES OF THE SAME COLOR ON THE TASSELS
FOR ADDED "POP."

1 Gather all of the materials and tools listed.

2 Copy shapes A, B, C, and D from template 12 on a separate sheet of paper. Then cut out the shapes using a cutting blade or scissors. Shapes A and B are used once, and shapes C and D are to be cut out five times to create tassels. Punch out the holes marked on the template shapes.

3 Place all shapes A and B on top of the leather, and cut around using the template as a guide.

MATERIALS

- Template 12 (page 109)
- Leather
- 8 jump rings, 6 mm
- 3 jump rings, 4 mm
- 20 inches (50.8 cm) of necklace chain
- 1 lobster clasp

TOOLS

- 1 cutting knife
- Cutting blades
- 1 cutting mat
- 1 disappearing fabric marker
- 1 ruler
- 2 chain-nose pliers
- 1 wire-cutter pliers
- 1 rotary hole punch
- Cyanoacrylate glue Leather bond glue

4 Place shapes C and D over the leather, and cut five of each.

6 Punch through each mark on shapes A and B using the rotary hole punch. Place the leather under the smallest hole, and squeeze to pierce through the leather. Continue to punch all nine holes.

5 Use a disappearing fabric marker to mark all small circles of the template onto the leather. These marks serve as a guide for the next step.

7 Start making the tassels using shape C. On each of the tassel pieces, measure down ⅛ inch (3 mm) from the top edge, and, with a disappearing fabric marker, make a row of marks 1/16 inch (1.5 mm) apart along this line. Next mark a corresponding set of 1/16-inch (1.5 mm) marks along the bottom edge. Cut the tassels beginning at the top mark and cutting through the bottom of the shape. Use a ruler to make sure the cuts are parallel and straight. Make sure not to mark or cut all the way to the top edge because a top strip is needed to roll the piece into a tassel in future steps. Repeat using the remaining C shapes to create five tassels.

8 Working on the back side of the leather, align one short end of shape B on the top right edge of the tassel cutout, and use cyanoacrylate glue to adhere. Fold shape D in half to create a loop and glue again. The loop is used to connect the jump ring to the tassel.

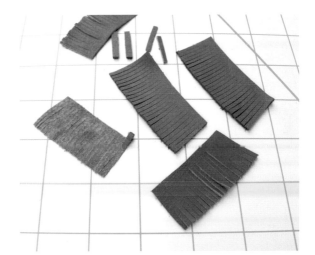

9 On the back side of the leather, spread a narrow band of leather bond glue along the top edge of the tassel cutout stopping ¼ inch (6 mm) from the end. This helps to strengthen the tassel. Hold the top of the loop, and roll tightly to create the tassel. Keep rolling until ¼ inch (6 mm) is left. Add cyanoacrylate glue to the end, and finish rolling. The glue will help keep the tassel from unrolling.

10 Repeat steps 8 and 9 to complete all five tassels.

11 Measure out two pieces of curb chain 10 inches (25.4 cm) long, and use the wire-cutter pliers to cut each piece.

12 Begin to assemble the necklace by attaching the leather tassels to the holes in shape A with 6-mm jump rings. Use the chain-nose pliers to open and close the jump rings.

14 Using two 4-mm jump rings, attach each of the 10-inch (25.4 cm) necklace chain pieces to the 6-mm rings used to join shapes A and B. To finish the necklace, use a 4-mm jump ring to attach a lobster clasp on one side. Add a 6-mm jump ring to the end of the other chain.

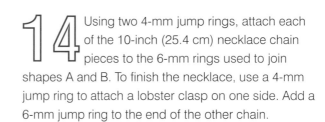

13 Attach shape B over shape A using the top two holes. Use chain-nose pliers and 6-mm jump rings to connect the pieces.

LEATHER TASSEL NECKLACE

—✂—

THIS NECKLACE IS A SIMPLE DESIGN OF STRINGING
TASSELS ALONG A SINGLE NECKLACE CHAIN.
ALTHOUGH THE ASSEMBLY IS SIMPLE, THE
EFFECT CAN MAKE A BIG STATEMENT. HAVE FUN
WITH THE COLORS OF LEATHER TO MAKE
THE DESIGN STAND OUT.

1 Gather all of the materials and tools listed. For this project I chose five different colors of leather for a festive look. Choosing bright shades of leather will make the necklace really unique. For a more subtle look, choose one color for all five tassels.

2 Copy shapes A and B from template 13 on a separate sheet of paper. Then cut out the shapes using a cutting blade or scissors. Cut each shape five times to create five tassels.

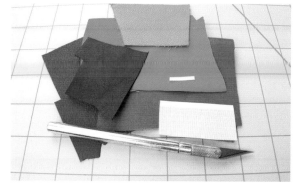

3 Place shapes A and B over the leather, and cut around to create five of each shape.

MATERIALS

- Template 13 (page 110)
- Leather
- 1 jump ring, 6 mm
- 6 jump rings, 4 mm
- 18 inches (45.7 cm) of necklace chain
- 1 lobster clasp

TOOLS

- 1 cutting knife
- Cutting blades
- 1 cutting mat
- 1 disappearing fabric marker
- 1 ruler
- 2 chain-nose pliers
- 1 wire-cutter pliers
- Cyanoacrylate glue
- Leather bond glue

4 On each of the five shape A tassel pieces, measure down ⅛ inch (3 mm) from the top edge, and, with a disappearing fabric marker, make a row of marks 1⁄16 inch (1.5 mm) apart along this line. Next mark a corresponding set of 1⁄16-inch (1.5 mm) marks along the bottom edge. Cut the tassels beginning at the top mark and cutting through the bottom of the shape. Use a ruler to make sure the cuts are parallel and straight. Make sure not to mark or cut all the way to the top edge because a top strip is needed to roll the piece into a tassel in future steps.

5 Working on the back side of the leather, align one short end of shape B on the top right edge of the tassel cutout, and use cyanoacrylate glue to adhere. Fold shape B in half to create a loop, and glue again. The loop is used to connect the jump ring to the tassel.

6 On the back side of the leather, spread a narrow band of leather bond glue along the top edge of the tassel cutout stopping ¼ inch (6 mm) from the end. This helps to strengthen the tassel. Hold the top of the loop, and roll tightly to create the tassel. Keep rolling until ¼ inch (6 mm) is left. Add cyanoacrylate glue to the end, and finish rolling. The glue will help keep the tassel from unrolling.

7 Repeat steps 5 and 6 to complete all five tassels.

10 Continue adding the leather tassels using 4-mm jump rings on each side of the centered tassel until all five are strung symmetrically on the chain.

8 Use a 4-mm jump ring and the two chain-nose pliers to attach one tassel in the middle of the 18-inch (45.7 cm) necklace chain.

11 Attach the lobster clasp on one end of the chain using a 4-mm jump ring, and attach a 6-mm jump ring on the other end of the chain.

9 After the first tassel is placed at the 9-inch (22.9 cm) mark of the chain, add two more tassels to the left and right sides at 1 inch (2.5 cm) intervals.

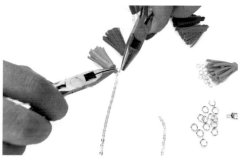

TRIANGLE LEATHER NECKLACE

CUT MULTIPLE SHAPES FROM VARIOUS COLORED
LEATHER TO CREATE A STATEMENT NECKLACE.
HAND-CUT GEOMETRIC EMBELLISHMENTS WILL BE
ATTACHED WITH JUMP RINGS FOR ADDED STYLE

1   Gather all of the materials and tools listed.

2   Copy shapes A, B, C, and D from template 14 on a separate sheet of paper. Then cut out the shapes using a cutting blade or scissors. Punch out all the holes marked on the shapes.

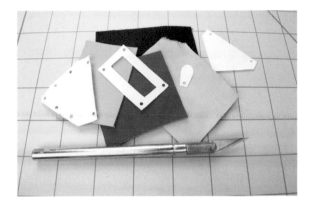

3   Place the templates on top of the leather, and trace around using a cutting blade. Shapes A, B, and C are cut out once, and shape D is cut out five times.

MATERIALS

- Template 14 (page 110)
- Leather
- 10 jump rings, 6 mm
- 1 jump ring, 4 mm
- 20 inches (50.8 cm) of necklace chain
- 1 lobster clasp

TOOLS

- 1 cutting knife
- Cutting blades
- 1 cutting mat
- 1 disappearing fabric marker
- 1 ruler
- 2 chain-nose pliers
- 1 wire-cutting pliers
- 1 rotary hole punch

4 Use a disappearing fabric marker to mark all the small circles of the template onto the leather. The marks will be punched out in the next step.

5 Punch through each mark on shapes A, B, C, and D using the rotary hole punch. Place the leather under the smallest hole, and squeeze to pierce through the leather. Continue to punch all 18 holes.

6 Use wire-cutting pliers and a ruler to measure out and cut two pieces of necklace chain, 10 inches (25.4 cm) long.

7 Use 6-mm jump rings and two chain-nose pliers to assemble shapes A, B, and C. Shape B is on the bottom, shape C is on top of shape B, and shape A is above them aligned along the top edge.

8 Lastly, attach the five shape Ds to the bottom of shape B using 6-mm jump rings.

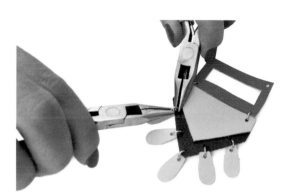

9 On the left and right holes at the top of shape A, attach the two pieces of necklace chain, one on each side, using two 6-mm jump rings. To finish the necklace attach one 4-mm jump ring with a lobster clasp on the end of one chain, and attach a 6-mm jump ring on the end of the other chain.

GEOMETRIC LEATHER NECKLACE
WITH BEADS AND FEATHERS

FEATHERS AND BEADS ARE MY FAVORITE MATERIALS
TO INCORPORATE INTO LEATHER CRAFT TO LIVEN
UP ANY DESIGN. MAKE A GEOMETRIC STATEMENT
NECKLACE, AND COMBINE BEADING AND FEATHERS
FOR THE ULTIMATE STATEMENT PIECE.

Gather all of the materials and tools listed.

 Copy shapes A, B, and C from template 15 on a separate sheet of paper. Then cut out the shapes using a cutting blade or scissors. This project requires one of each template shape. Punch out the holes marked on each shape.

Place the template shapes over the leather, and cut around each using a cutting blade or scissors.

MATERIALS

- Template 15 (page 110)
- Leather
- 6 jump rings, 6 mm
- 5 jump rings, 4 mm
- 3 feathers
- 3 crimp ends
- 6 heishi howlite beads
- 4 seed beads, 8 mm
- 4 turquoise irregular chip beads
- 2 eye pins, 1 inch (2.5 cm)
- Necklace chain, 20 inches (50.8 cm) long
- 1 lobster clasp

TOOLS

- 1 cutting knife
- Cutting blades
- 1 cutting mat
- 1 disappearing fabric marker
- 1 ruler
- 2 chain-nose pliers
- 1 round-nose pliers
- 1 wire-cutter pliers
- 1 rotary hole punch

4 Use a disappearing fabric marker to mark all the hole punch circles of the template onto the leather.

5 Punch through each mark on shapes A, B, and C using the rotary hole punch. Place the leather under the smallest hole, and squeeze to pierce through the leather. Punch all nine holes.

6 To create the beaded part of the necklace, onto each 1-inch (2.5 cm) eye pin string 3 heishi howlite beads, 2 (8-mm) seed beads, and 2 turquoise irregular chip beads.

7 Use round-nose pliers to bend the pins at a 90-degree angle. With wire-cutter pliers trim the excess metal until there is about ¼ inch (6 mm) left.

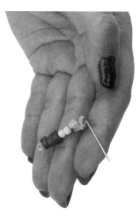

8 Create a loop using the round-nose pliers. The beaded eye pins now have a loop at each end that is used to connect the necklace chain to the leather ornament.

9 To prepare the feathers, trim the top of the feather stem using a cutting blade. There are many different types and colors of feathers that will work great for this project. I chose three different colors of goose feathers.

10 Add a small amount of glue to the crimp end, and insert the feather stem. Use a pair of chain-nose pliers to push each end of the crimp end in to close over the stem.

11 Attach each of the three feathers to the bottom three holes in shape A using 6-mm jump rings and two chain-nose pliers.

12 Attach shapes A, B, and C together with two 6-mm jump rings. Position the pieces with shape A on the bottom, shape B on top of shape A, and shape C on top of shape B, aligning the holes punched in each of the shapes.

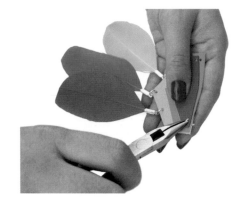

13 Use a 4-mm jump ring to connect the beaded eye pins to the top left and right 6-mm jump rings that were used to join shapes A, B, and C together. Next, attach the pieces of necklace chain, one to each of the connected eye pins, using two 4-mm jump rings.

14 To finish the necklace use a 4-mm jump ring to attach the lobster clasp to the end of one of the chains, and attach a 6-mm jump ring on the end of the other chain.

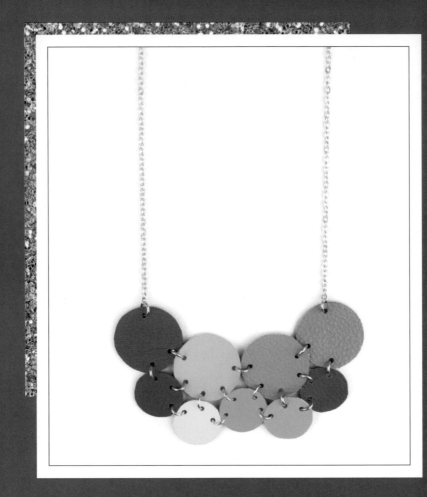

LEATHER CIRCLE NECKLACE

CREATE A NECKLACE BY COMBINING VARIOUS-SIZED
CIRCLES WITH JUMP RINGS. I LIKE TO USE DIFFERENT
SHADES OF LEATHER FOR EACH CUTOUT SHAPE.
FOR A MORE SUBTLE LOOK, USE OMBRE SHADES OF
THE SAME COLOR WITH POPS OF METALLIC
LEATHER FOR A HIGH- END LOOK.

Gather all of the materials and tools listed.

2 Copy shapes A, B, C, D, E, F, G, H, and I from template 16 on a separate sheet of paper. Then cut out the shapes using a cutting blade or scissors. Punch out the holes as marked on the template shapes.

3 Cut out each shape once, for a total of nine circles. Place the shapes over the leather, and cut out using the template as a guide.

MATERIALS

- Template 16 (page 111)
- Leather
- 18 jump rings, 6 mm
- 1 jump ring, 4 mm
- Necklace chain, 18 inches (45.7 cm)
- 1 lobster clasp

TOOLS

- 1 cutting knife
- Cutting blades
- 1 cutting mat
- 1 disappearing fabric marker
- 2 chain-nose pliers
- 1 ruler
- 1 wire-cutter pliers
- 1 rotary hole punch

4 Use a disappearing fabric marker to mark the hole cutouts on each template.

5 Punch through each mark on all nine circles using the rotary hole punch. Place the leather under the smallest hole, and squeeze to pierce through the leather. Continue to punch until all 32 holes are cut.

6 Start assembling the necklace by attaching shapes A, E, and B using the two pairs of chain-nose pliers and 6-mm jump rings. Refer to the original template image to understand the arrangement of the pieces. The orientation of the punched holes is very important in fitting the pieces together properly.

7 Continue to attach shapes B, F, G, C, and H in that order.

8 Finish the assembly by adding shapes D and I.

9 Use a ruler and the wire-cutter pliers to measure and cut two pieces of necklace chain 9 inches (22.9 cm) long.

10 Attach one chain segment to the top of shape A using the chain-nose pliers and a 6-mm jump ring. Repeat for the right side by adding the other chain segment to the top of shape D.

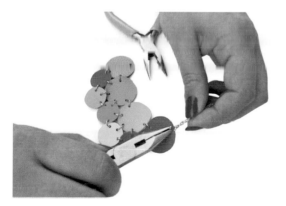

11 Add the lobster clasp to the end of one chain using a 4-mm jump ring. Attach a 6-mm jump ring to the end of the other chain to complete the necklace.

VARIATION: GEOMETRIC NECKLACE

THIS IS A GREAT VARIATION TO THE LEATHER CIRCLE
NECKLACE. USE VARIOUS-SHAPED GEOMETRIC
LEATHER SHAPES ATTACHED WITH JUMP RINGS. THE
FUN PART OF THIS PROJECT IS THE RANDOMNESS OF
THE SHAPES THAT FIT TOGETHER IN AN INTERESTING
COMPOSITION. THIS DESIGN IS SURE TO BE A
CONVERSATION STARTER.

Gather all of the materials and tools listed.

Copy shapes A, B, C, D, E, F, and G from template 17 on a separate sheet of paper. Then cut out the shapes using a cutting blade or scissors. Punch out the holes marked on the template shapes. This project requires one copy of each template shape.

Place each of the seven shapes over the leather, and cut out using a cutting blade.

MATERIALS

- Template 17 (page 111)
- Leather
- 18 jump rings, 6 mm
- 1 jump ring, 4 mm
- 18 inches (45.7 cm) of necklace chain
- 1 lobster clasp

TOOLS

- 1 cutting knife
- Cutting blades
- 1 cutting mat
- 1 disappearing fabric marker
- 2 chain-nose pliers
- 1 ruler
- 1 wire-cutter pliers
- 1 rotary hole punch

4 Use a disappearing fabric marker to mark each small hole in the templates onto the leather. These holes will be punched in the next step.

5 Punch through each mark on all seven shapes using the rotary hole punch. Place the leather under the smallest hole, and squeeze to pierce through the leather. Continue to punch until all 32 holes are cut.

6 To begin assembling the leather pieces into a necklace, refer to the sequence of the pieces as they appear in the template, and lay them out in order.

7 Attach shape A to shape B using two pairs of chain-nose pliers and 6-mm jump rings.

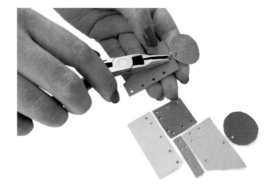

8 Continue to attach shapes C and D to shape B with 6-mm jump rings. Next attach shapes E and F to shapes C and D. Lastly add shape G to shape F.

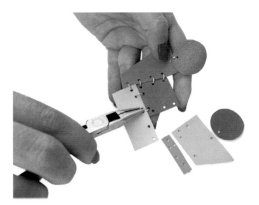

10 Attach one chain segment to the top of shape A using a pair of chain-nose pliers and a 6-mm jump ring. Attach the second chain to the top of shape G with another 6-mm jump ring.

9 Use the ruler and wire-cutter pliers to measure and cut two pieces of necklace chain 9 inches (22.9 cm) long.

11 Finish the necklace by attaching the lobster clasp to the end of one of the chains using a 4-mm jump ring. Attach a 6-mm jump ring to the end of the other chain.

FRINGE LAYERED LEATHER NECKLACE

CREATE A LAYERED LEATHER FRINGE NECKLACE. UP TO
FOUR DIFFERENT COLORED LEATHERS CAN BE CUT INTO
FRINGE FOR A BRIGHT AND DARING LOOK.

1 Gather all of the materials and tools listed.

2 Copy shapes A, B, C, and D from template 18 on a separate sheet of paper. Then cut out the shapes using a cutting blade or scissors. Punch out all the holes marked on the template shapes. This project will require one copy of each template shape.

3 Put each template on top of the leather, and cut out using a cutting blade.

MATERIALS

- Template 18 (page 112)
- Leather
- 3 jump rings, 6 mm
- 3 jump rings, 4 mm
- 20 inches (50.8 cm) of necklace chain
- 1 lobster clasp

TOOLS

- 1 cutting knife
- Cutting blades
- 1 cutting mat
- 1 disappearing fabric marker
- 2 chain-nose pliers
- 1 ruler
- 1 wire-cutter pliers
- 1 rotary hole punch

4 Use a disappearing fabric marker to mark the hole cutouts on each template shape. The marks tell where to punch the holes in the next step.

5 Punch through each mark on all four shapes using the rotary hole punch. Place the leather under the smallest hole, and squeeze to pierce through the leather. Continue to punch until all eight holes are cut.

6 To make the fringe pieces, on shape A, measure down ⅛ inch (3 mm) from the top edge, and make a row of marks ¹⁄₁₆ inch (1.5 mm) apart along this line. Next mark a corresponding set of ¹⁄₁₆-inch (1.5 mm) marks along the bottom edge. Cut the fringe beginning at the top mark and cutting through the bottom of the shape. Use a ruler to make sure the cuts are parallel and straight. Make sure not to mark or cut all the way to the top edge.

7 For shapes B, C, and D, measure down ¼ inch (6 mm) from the top edge to make the row of ¹⁄₁₆-inch (1.5 mm) marks. Continue to make the shapes B, C, and D fringe following the remaining instructions used for shape A.

8 Use the ruler and wire-cutter pliers to measure and cut two pieces of necklace chain 10 inches (25.4 cm) long.

9 Assemble the necklace by attaching shapes A, B, C, and D with two 6-mm jump rings and two chain-nose pliers. Stack the shapes one on top of the other with the holes aligned. Place shape D on the bottom, shape C next, shape B on top of shape C, and shape A on the very top.

10 Attach one chain segment to the top left 6-mm jump ring using the chain-nose pliers and a 4-mm jump ring. Attach the second chain to the top right 6-mm jump ring with another 4-mm jump ring.

11 Finish the necklace by attaching the lobster clasp to the end of one of the chains, and attach a 6-mm jump ring to the end of the other chain.

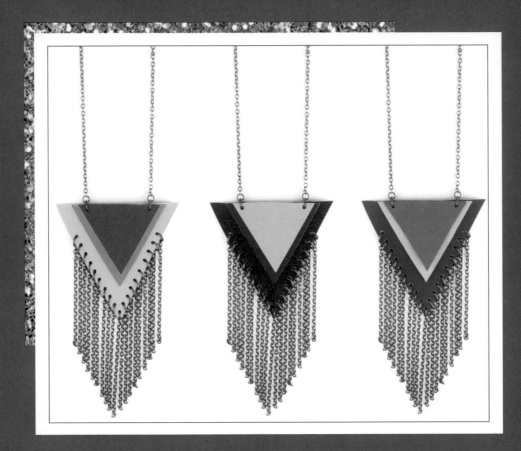

DANGLING CHAIN
TRIANGLE NECKLACE

THIS DESIGN USES A SIMPLE TRIANGLE GEOMETRIC
CUTOUT SHAPE AS THE BASE OF THE NECKLACE,
WITH THE FOCUS BEING ON THE DANGLING CHAIN
ELEMENTS. HANGING OFF THE TRIANGLE WILL BE 19
CHAINS ATTACHED WITH JUMP RINGS. THIS NECKLACE
IS A FUN STATEMENT PIECE.

Gather all of the materials and tools listed.

2 Copy shapes A, B, and C from template 19 on a separate sheet of paper. Then cut out the shapes using a cutting blade or scissors. The project will require one of each for a total of three shapes. Punch out the holes marked on each of the shapes.

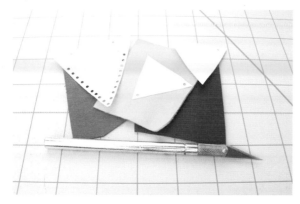

3 Put all three shapes on top of the leather, and cut around using the template as a guide.

4 Use a disappearing fabric marker to mark the hole cutouts on each template. These marks show where to punch the holes in the next step.

6 Using the ruler and wire-cutter pliers, measure and cut two segments of chain 10 inches (25.4 cm) long.

5 Punch through each mark on all four shapes using the rotary hole punch. Place the leather under the smallest hole, and squeeze to pierce through the leather. Continue to punch until all 25 holes are cut.

7 Next, use the ruler and wire-cutter pliers to cut 19 pieces of necklace chain 2 inches (5.1 cm) long. The 19 segments of 2-inch (5.1 cm) chain will dangle below shape A.

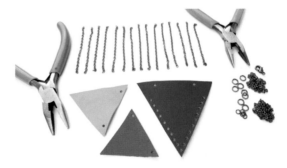

8 Attach one of the 2-inch (5.1 cm) chains to each of the holes running along the sides of shape A using two chain-nose pliers and 6-mm jump rings.

9 Stack shapes A, B, and C aligning the holes at the top of each leather piece. Place shape A on the bottom, shape B in the middle, and shape C on the top. Using 6-mm jump rings, join the pieces together.

10 Attach one 10-inch (25.4 cm) chain segment to the top left 6-mm jump ring using a pair of chain-nose pliers and a 4-mm jump ring. Add the second chain to the top right with another 4-mm jump ring. Lastly, finish the necklace by attaching one 4-mm jump ring with a lobster clasp on the end of the chain and attach a 6-mm jump ring on the other end of the chain.

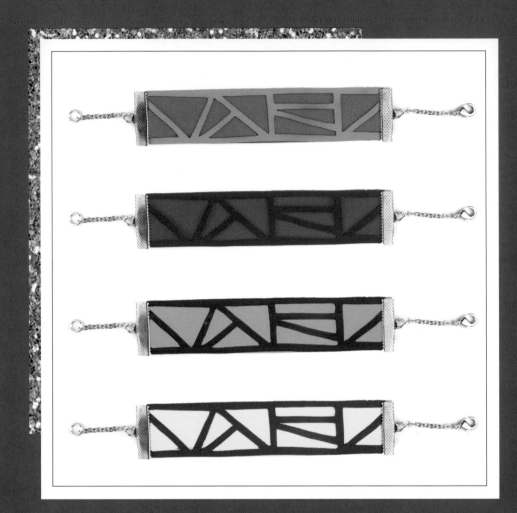

GEOMETRIC CUFF BRACELET

BRACELETS ARE A GREAT WAY TO ADD COLOR TO
YOUR EVERYDAY LOOK. CREATE A GEOMETRIC
LATTICE BRACELET LAYERED OVER A BRIGHT
LEATHER BACK PIECE.

Gather all of the materials and tools listed.

2 Copy shapes A and B from template 20 on a separate sheet of paper. Then cut out the shapes using a cutting blade or scissors. This project requires one copy of each template shape.

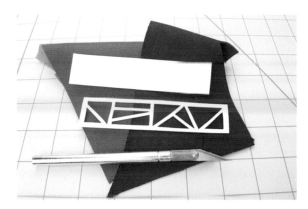

3 Place shape A over the leather, and trace the outer rectangle border. The internal lattice will be cut in step 5.

MATERIALS

- Template 20 (page 113)
- Leather
- 2 ribbon ends, 1 inch (2.5 cm)
- 3 jump rings, 6 mm
- 1 jump ring, 4 mm
- 2 segments of chain, 1 inch (2.5 cm) long
- 1 lobster clasp

TOOLS

- 1 cutting knife
- Cutting blades
- 1 cutting mat
- 2 chain-nose pliers
- 1 ruler
- 1 wire-cutter pliers
- Cyanoacrylate glue

4 Cut out shape B by placing the template over the leather and cutting around it using a cutting blade. Shape B is the solid piece that sits under shape A.

6 Continue to cut each section, and replace the blade as needed to get precise cuts. If the pattern is too difficult to cut out, choose only a few shapes to cut.

5 Carefully cut out the larger sections of the geometric lattice pattern in shape A using the template and a cutting blade.

7 Add cyanoacrylate glue to the ends of shape B and place shape A on top. The glue will help with the insertion into the ribbon ends.

8 To add the ribbon ends, insert one end of the leather into one of the ribbon ends. Use the chain-nose pliers to clamp down evenly along the ribbon end. Repeat for the other end. A small amount of additional cyanoacrylate placed inside the ribbon end before inserting the leather can reinforce the hold.

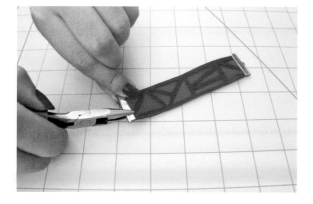

9 Use a ruler and the wire-cutter pliers to measure and cut two segments of chain 1 inch (2.5 cm) long.

10 Attach one of the chain segments to the small hole in one of the ribbon ends using two chain-nose pliers and a 6-mm jump ring. Repeat for the other side.

11 Attach the lobster clasp to the end of one of the chains using a 4-mm jump ring. Attach a 6-mm jump ring to the end of the other chain.

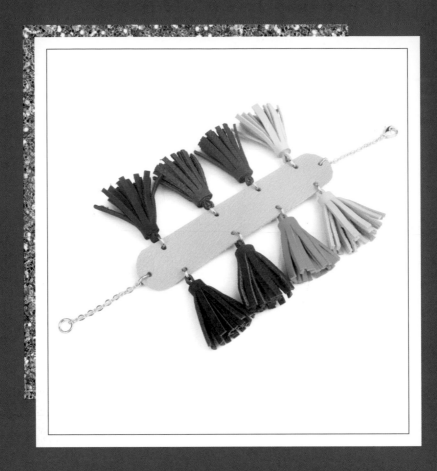

LEATHER TASSEL BRACELET

CREATE A BOLD AND STYLISH TASSEL BRACELET. MY
FAVORITE PART OF THIS PROJECT IS THAT YOU CAN
CHOOSE UP TO EIGHT DIFFERENT COLORED TASSELS
FOR A UNIQUE LOOK. FOR A MORE SUBTLE LOOK,
CHOOSE SHADES OF THE SAME HUE OR MAKE THE
TASSELS ALL THE SAME COLOR.

Gather all of the materials and tools listed.

2 Copy shapes A, B, and C from template 21 on a separate sheet of paper. Then cut out the shapes using a cutting blade or scissors This project requires one cutout of shape A and eight cutouts of shapes B and C. Punch out the holes as marked on the template shapes.

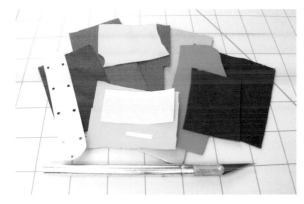

3 Place shape A on top of the leather, and cut out using a cutting blade.

MATERIALS

- Template 21 (page 113)
- Leather
- 11 jump rings, 6 mm
- 1 jump ring, 4 mm
- 2 segments of chain, 1 1/4 inch (3.2 cm) long
- 1 lobster clasp

TOOLS

- 1 cutting knife
- Cutting blades
- 1 cutting mat
- 1 disappearing fabric marker
- 1 ruler
- 2 chain-nose pliers
- 1 wire-cutter pliers
- 1 rotary hole punch
- Cyanoacrylate glue
- Leather bond glue

4 Use a disappearing fabric marker to mark the hole cutouts on each template. The marks show where to punch the holes in the next step.

5 Punch through each mark on shape A using the rotary hole punch. Place the leather under the smallest hole, and squeeze to pierce through the leather. Continue to punch until all 10 holes are cut.

6 On each of the shape B pieces, measure down ⅛ inch (3 mm) from the top edge, and make a row of marks ¹⁄₁₆ inch (1.5 mm) apart along this line. Next mark a corresponding set of ¹⁄₁₆-inch (1.5 mm) marks along the bottom edge. Cut the tassels beginning at the top mark and cutting through the bottom of the shape. Use a ruler to make sure the cuts are parallel and straight. Do not mark or cut to all the way to the top edge because a top strip is needed to roll the piece into a tassel in future steps.

7 Working on the back side of the leather, align one short end of shape B on the top left edge of the tassel cutout, and use cyanoacrylate glue to adhere. Fold shape B in half to create a loop and glue again. The loop is used to connect the jump ring and tassel to the bracelet.

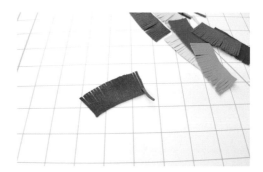

8 On the back side of the leather, spread a narrow band of leather bond glue along the top edge of the tassel cutout stopping ¼ inch (6 mm) from the end. This helps to strengthen the tassel. Hold the top of the loop, and roll tightly to create the tassel. Keep rolling until ¼ inch (6 mm) is left. Add cyanoacrylate glue to the end, and finish rolling. The glue will help keep the tassel from unrolling.

9 Repeat steps 6, 7, and 8 to complete all eight tassels.

10 Use the ruler and wire-cutter pliers to measure and cut two segments of chain 1¼ inch (3.2 cm) long.

11 Attach a tassel to shape A using 6-mm jump rings and two chain-nose pliers. Continue to add all eight tassels to the sides of shape A.

12 Use a 6-mm jump ring to attach one of the 1¼ inches (3.2 cm) chains to each end of shape A.

13 To finish the bracelet, attach the lobster clasp with a 4-mm jump ring on the end of one of the chains. Attach a 6-mm jump ring on the end of the other chain.

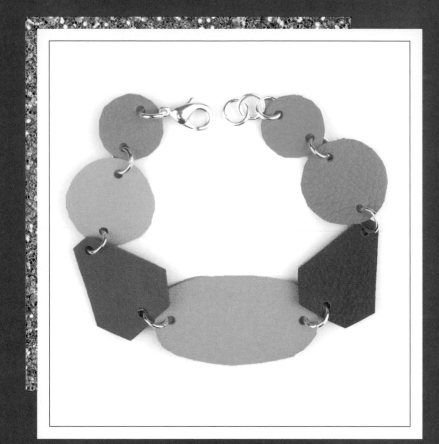

1 Gather all of the materials and tools listed.

2 Copy shapes A, B, C, D, E, F, and G from template 22 on a separate sheet of paper. Then cut out the shapes using a cutting blade or scissors. This project requires one cutout of each template shape. Punch out the holes as marked on the shapes.

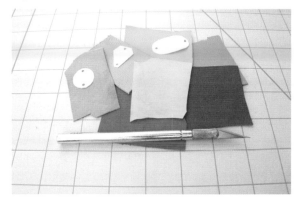

3 Place all seven template shapes on top of the leather, and cut around using a cutting blade.

MATERIALS

- Template 22 (page 113)
- Leather
- 9 jump rings, 6 mm
- 1 jump ring, 4 mm
- 1 lobster clasp

TOOLS

- 1 cutting knife
- Cutting blades
- 1 cutting mat
- 1 disappearing fabric marker
- 2 chain-nose pliers
- 1 rotary hole punch

4 Use a disappearing fabric marker to mark the hole cutouts on each template shape.

5 Punch through each mark on all seven shapes using the rotary hole punch. Place the leather under the smallest hole, and squeeze to pierce through the leather. Continue to punch until all 14 holes are cut.

6 Lay out all the shapes in the order they are to be positioned for the bracelet design.

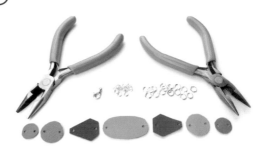

7 Attach the leather pieces using 6-mm jump rings and two chain-nose pliers. Assemble the pieces in order starting with shape A attaching to shape B, shape B attaching to shape C, shape C to shape D, shape D to shape E, shape E to shape F, and lastly shape F to shape G.

8 At one end of the bracelet, attach the lobster clasp using a 4-mm jump ring. At the other end attach a 6-mm jump ring.

TEMPLATES

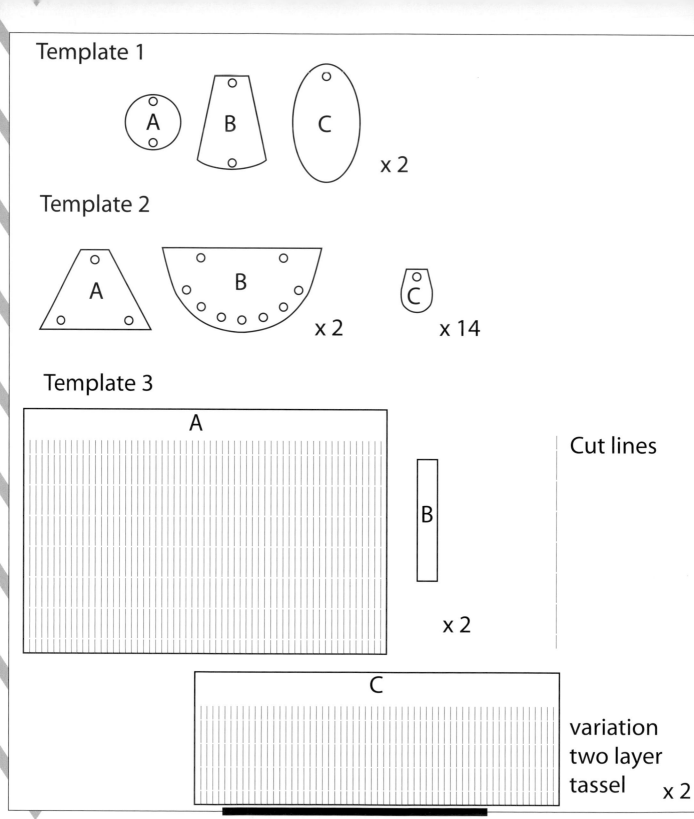

Template 1

A

B

C

x 2

Template 2

A

B

C

x 2

x 14

Template 3

A

B

Cut lines

x 2

C

variation
two layer
tassel

x 2

Template 4

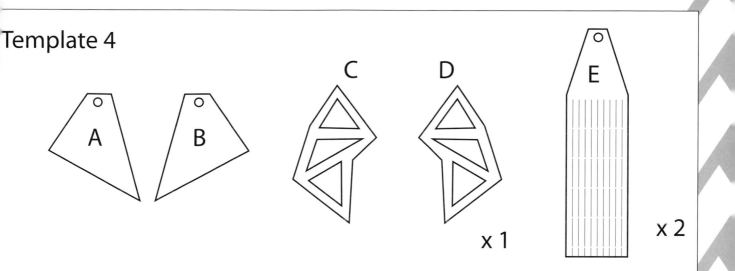

A   B   C   D   E

x 1

x 2

Template 5

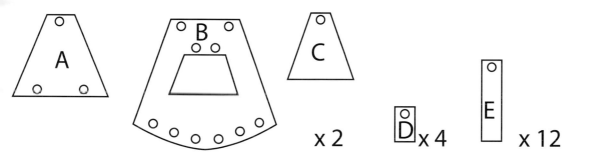

A   B   C

x 2

D x 4

E x 12

Template 6

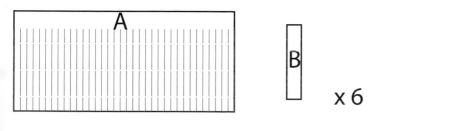

A

B

x 6

Cut lines

Template 7

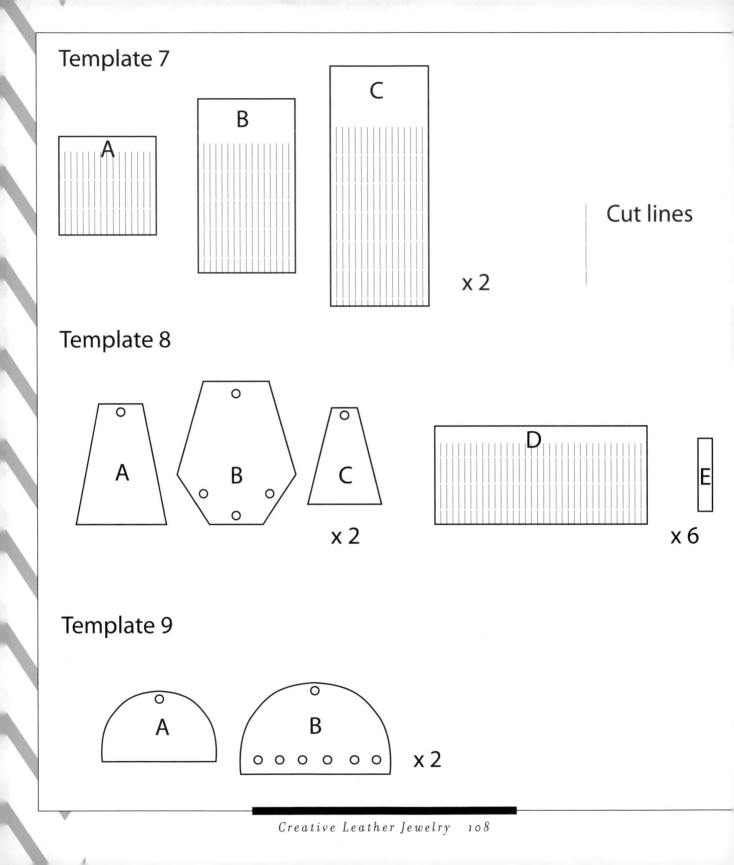

A

B

C

x 2

Cut lines

Template 8

A

B

C

x 2

D

E

x 6

Template 9

A

B

x 2

Template 10

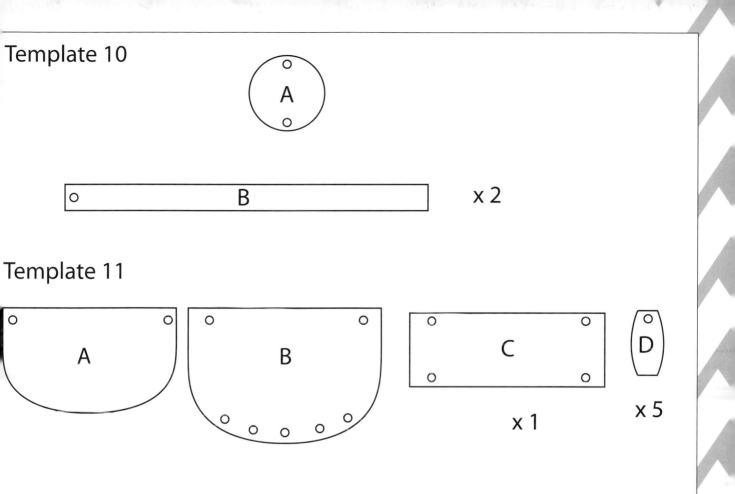

A

B x 2

Template 11

A

B

C x 1

D x 5

Template 12

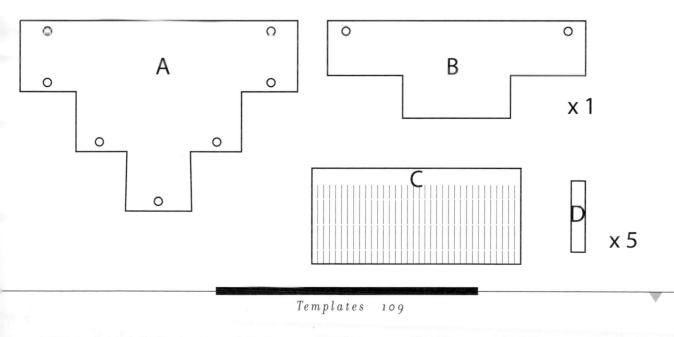

A

B x 1

C

D x 5

Template 13

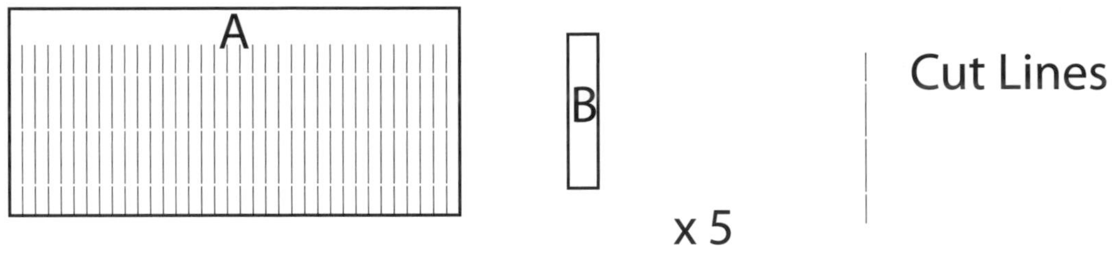

A

B   Cut Lines

x 5

Template 14

A

B

C

D

x 1   x 5

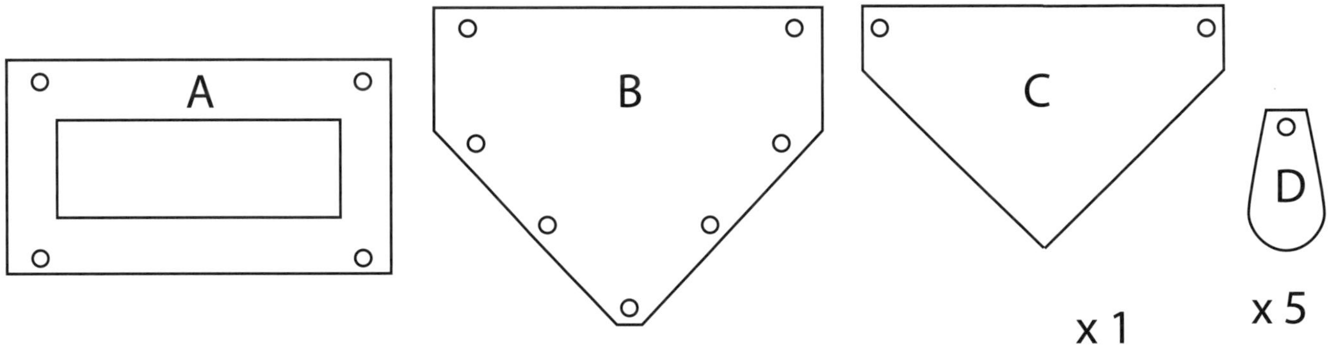

Template 15

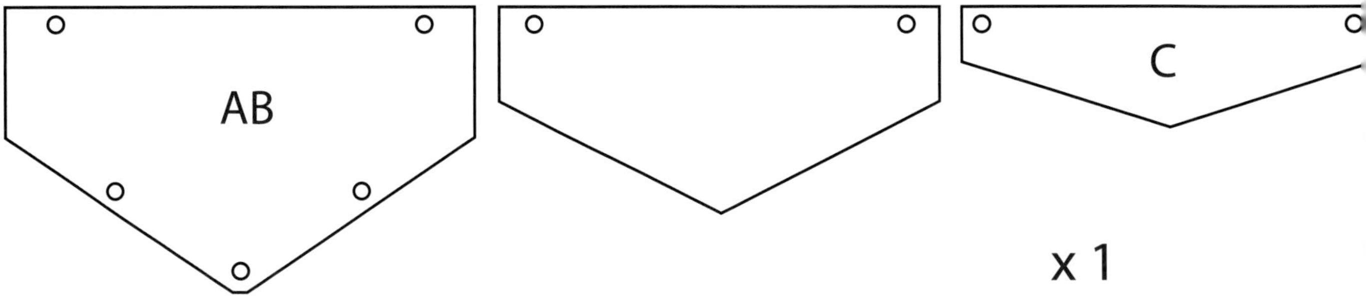

AB

C

x 1

Template 16

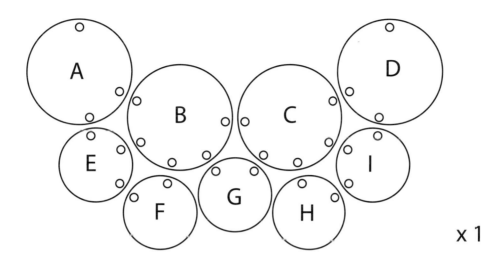

x 1

Template 17

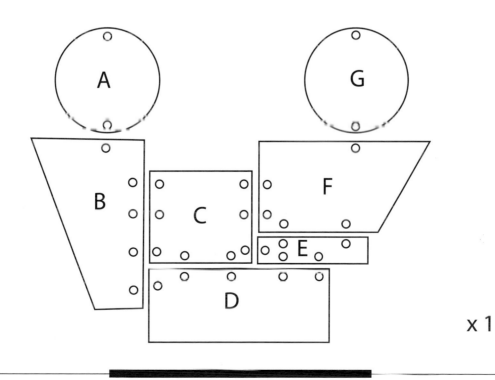

x 1

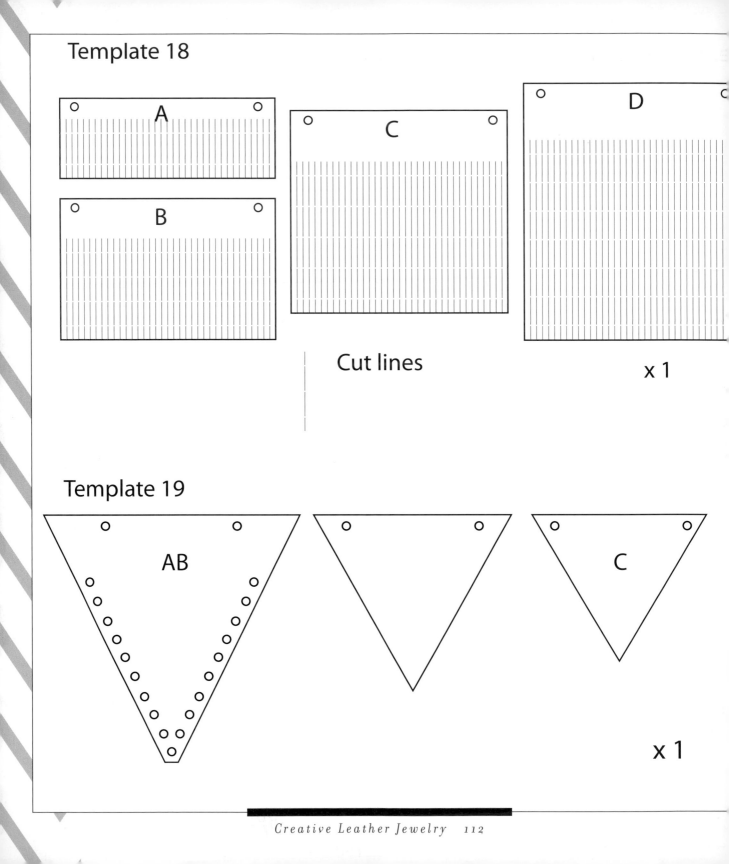

Template 18

A

B

C

D

Cut lines

x 1

Template 19

AB

C

x 1

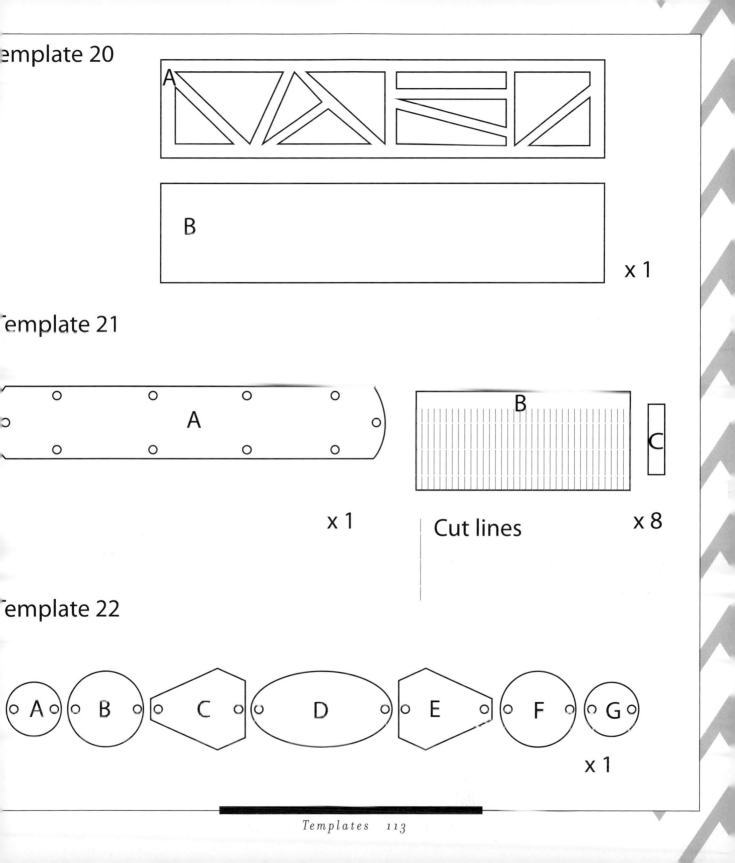

Template 20

A

B

x 1

Template 21

A

x 1

B

C

Cut lines

x 8

Template 22

A B C D E F G

x 1

ACKNOWLEDGMENTS

A special thank you to Lark Crafts and Sterling Publishing for adding me to their family of amazing authors. I'm honored to be able to share my craft and my passion through this book.

To my friends and family for all of your support and encouragement of my creative endeavors.

I want to thank all of my fellow creatives for their support and inspiration. I have met so many amazing handmade artists who have turned their passion into successful small businesses. Sharing knowledge and building a community of like-minded entrepreneurs has helped me to keep growing, personally and professionally.

I also would like to thank everyone who has purchased my jewelry and supported Boo and Boo Factory. Without you I would not be able to do what I love for a living.

INDEX

ABOUT THE AUTHOR

CHRISTINA ANTON has a bachelor's degree in architecture from the University of Illinois at Chicago and a master's in architecture from the Southern California Institute of Architecture. While she pursued her degrees, she began Boo and Boo Factory as a hands-on creative outlet that supplemented her architectural ideas. Inspired by creating for a living, she took her growing jewelry design business and pursued it full time.

Christina lives in Chicago, where she works full time on her jewelry and accessories label Boo and Boo Factory. Having worked as an architectural designer in New York, Chicago, and Los Angeles, it was easy to take her love of shapes, colors, patterns, and textures and create beautiful one-of-a-kind jewelry pieces. She specializes in statement necklaces, bold neon earrings, bright color bracelets, wallets, and bags, which combine techniques ranging from hand-painting, hand-cut, beaded, and woven materials. She incorporates mixed media materials such as patterned leather, lambskin, cow hide, brass findings, gemstones, silicone tubing, and vintage beads.

Website: http://booandboofactory.com
Shop: http://shop.booandboofactory.com
Instagram: https://instagram.com/booandboofactory/
Facebook: https://www.facebook.com/BooandBooFactoryJewelry
Pinterest: https://www.pinterest.com/booanboofactory/